SCRATCH
CODE CHALLENGE

Scratch Code
ROBOTS

Max
Wainewright

CRABTREE
PUBLISHING COMPANY
WWW.CRABTREEBOOKS.COM

CRABTREE
PUBLISHING COMPANY
WWW.CRABTREEBOOKS.COM

Author: Max Wainewright

Editorial director: Kathy Middleton

Editors: Elise Short, Crystal Sikkens

Proofreader: Melissa Boyce

Design: Matt Lilly

Cover design: Peter Scoulding

Illustrations: John Haslam

Prepress technician: Margaret Amy Salter

Print coordinator: Katherine Berti

Every attempt has been made to clear copyright.
Should there be any inadvertent omission please
apply to the publisher for rectification.

Picture credits:
Shutterstock: NicoElNino 6, VCoscaron 12, petrmalinak
14, Andrey_Popov 18, Sean Pavone 24, Photographicss 28,
Dreamstime: GarcÃa Juan 26.

We recommend that children are supervised at all times when
using the Internet. Some of the projects in this series use a
computer webcam or microphone. Please make sure children are
made aware that they should only allow a computer to access
the webcam or microphone on specific websites that a trusted
adult has told them to use. We do not recommend children use
websites or microphones on any other websites other than those
mentioned in this book.

The website addresses (URLs) included in this book were valid at
the time of going to press. However, it is possible that contents or
addresses may have changed since the publication of this book.
No responsibility for any such changes can be accepted by either
the author or the Publisher.

Scratch is developed by the Lifelong Kindergarten Group at the
MIT Media Lab. See http://scratch.mit.edu.

Images and illustrations from Scratch included in this book have
been developed by the Lifelong Kindergarten Group at the MIT
Media Lab (see http://scratch.mit.edu) and made available
under the Creative Commons Attribution-ShareAlike 2.0 license
(https://creativecommons.org/licenses/by-sa/2.0/deed.en). The
third party trademarks used in this book are the property of their
respective owners, including the Scratch name and logo. The
owners of these trademarks have not endorsed, authorized or
sponsored this book.

Library and Archives Canada Cataloguing in Publication

Title: Scratch code robots / Max Wainewright.
Other titles: Robots
Names: Wainewright, Max, author.
Description: Series statement: Scratch code challenge |
  Includes index.
Identifiers: Canadiana (print) 20190107006 |
  Canadiana (ebook) 20190107154 |
  ISBN 9780778765325 (hardcover) |
  ISBN 9780778765677 (softcover) |
  ISBN 9781427123848 (HTML)
Subjects: LCSH: Robots—Computer programs—Juvenile
  literature. | LCSH: Scratch (Computer program language)—
  Juvenile literature. | LCSH: Computer programming—
  Juvenile literature.
Classification: LCC TJ211.2 .W35 2019 | DDC j629.8/92—dc23

Library of Congress Cataloging-in-Publication Data

Names: Wainewright, Max, author.
Title: Scratch code robots / Max Wainewright.
Other titles: Robots
Description: New York, New York : Crabtree Publishing, 2020. |
  Series: Scratch code challenge | "First published in Great Britain
  in 2019 by Wayland." | Includes index.
Identifiers: LCCN 2019013622 (print) | LCCN 2019014503 (ebook)
  ISBN 9781427123848 (Electronic) |
  ISBN 9780778765325 (hardcover : alk. paper) |
  ISBN 9780778765677 (pbk. : alk. paper)
Subjects: LCSH: Robots--Computer programs--Juvenile literature.
  | Scratch (Computer program language)--Juvenile literature. |
  Computer programming--Juvenile literature.
Classification: LCC TJ211.2 (ebook) |
  LCC TJ211.2 .W35 2020 (print) | DDC 629.8/92--dc23
LC record available at https://lccn.loc.gov/2019013622

Crabtree Publishing Company

www.crabtreebooks.com   1–800–387–7650

Published by Crabtree Publishing Company in 2020

Text copyright © ICT Apps, 2019
Art and design copyright © Hodder and Stoughton, 2019

Printed in the U.S.A./072019/CG20190501

Published in Canada
Crabtree Publishing
616 Welland Ave.
St. Catharines, Ontario
L2M 5V6

Published in the United States
Crabtree Publishing
PMB 59051
350 Fifth Avenue, 59th Floor
New York, New York 10118

Contents

Words in *italics* appear in the glossary on page 31.

Introduction

For thousands of years, people have created machines that could carry out tasks to help us. In the 1700s, inventors created "automatons," which were mechanical devices made to look like humans. They were able to carry out a series of movements or play a basic tune on an instrument. Relying on complex combinations of gears and levers, these early robots were mainly used as a form of entertainment. It wasn't until the 1940s that electronics were used to control and program robots. This led to the development of more sophisticated robots.

In this book, we'll look at how the different *systems* within robots work. We will see how they move around, sense where they are, and interact with us. You'll use the *algorithms* and ideas that control real robots to create your own on-screen robots. These programs will help you understand the world of robots and how they work.

There are a lot of different ways to create code. We will be using a website called Scratch to do our coding.

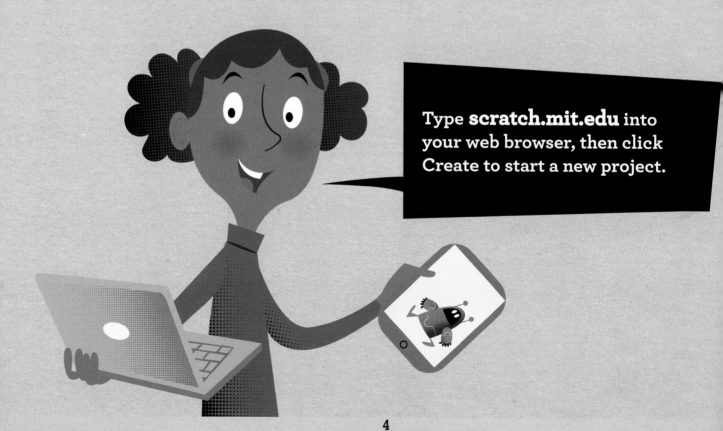

Type **scratch.mit.edu** into your web browser, then click **Create** to start a new project.

Let's start by looking at the important parts of the screen in Scratch:

File Menu (for logged-in users)
If you want, you can create an account for free and save your work online. Check with a grown-up first. Alternatively, you can use the Load and Save options to open and save work on your computer.

Sound Library
Add sounds to your program from here.

File Menu (for general users)
Choose Load and Save to open and save work on your computer.

New
Load from your computer
Save to your computer

New
Save Now
Save as a Copy
Go to My Stuff
Upload to your computer
Download to your computer
Record and Export Video
Revert

Block Categories
Choose commands from these categories.

List of Commands
Find the blocks you need by matching the color to the category name. For example, dark blue blocks will be found in the motion category.

Scripts Area
Add your commands or code here.

The Stage
Your program takes place on the *Stage*.

Sprites
Objects that move around in Scratch are called *sprites*.

Sprites Pane
Use this area to select which of your sprites you want to add code or sound to.

Sprite Library
Choose ready-made sprites for your programs.

Paint Editor
This is where you can draw your own sprites or backdrops.

Costume Pane

Drawing Tools

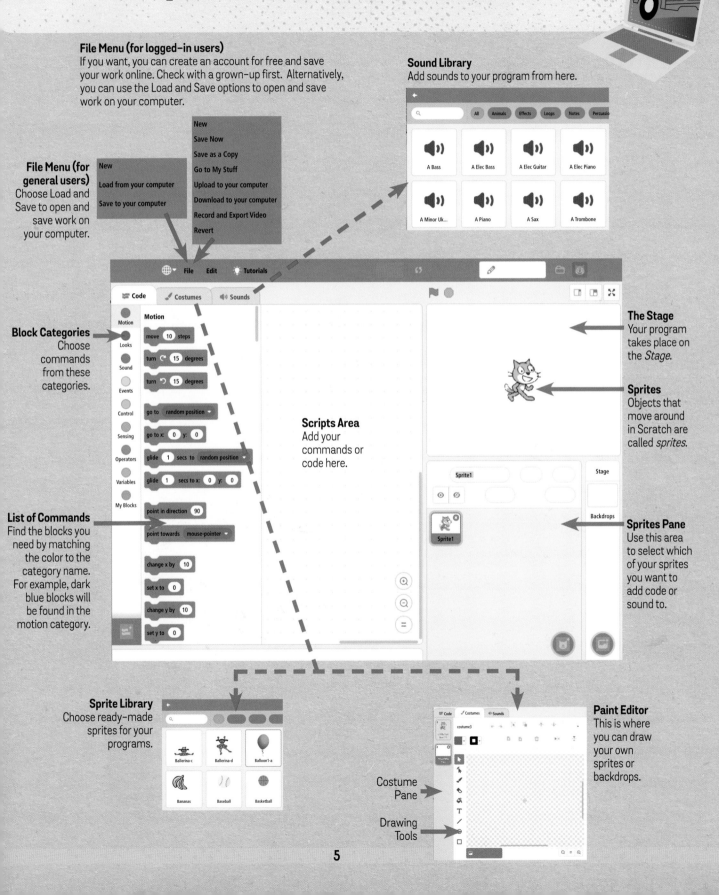

5

Following Instructions

We'll start off by looking at how a simple robot can be programmed to carry out a series of *steps*, one after another.

This is called a sequential program. If you don't have a robot handy, we'll draw one and create a maze for it to travel through.

For help, go to:
www.maxw.com

STEP 1 –
Remove the cat

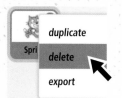

Right-click on the cat in the bottom right corner and click **delete**.

STEP 2 – **Add a sprite**

Hover over the **Choose a Sprite** button.

Click the **Brush** *icon*.

STEP 3 – Start drawing

Click **Convert to Bitmap**.

Select the **Rectangle** tool.

Set the rectangle to **Filled**.

Choose a color for your robot.

STEP 4 – Draw the robot

Start by dragging out a rectangle in the center of the drawing area. Make it about one-quarter of the width of the drawing area. (We'll draw it quite large so we can add detail, then shrink it in step 11.)

Click off the rectangle and then select a darker color.

Create two more rectangles to be the robot's arms.

STEP 5 – Eyes and details

Choose white, then draw two white rectangles to start creating the eyes.

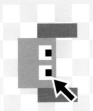

Select black, then add pupils to the eyes.

Add any other details you want to your robot.

Click the Undo tool if you make a mistake.

STEP 6 – The maze

 Click on the **Stage** icon next to the **Sprites** pane.

 Click the **Backdrops** tab.

 Click **Convert to Bitmap**.

STEP 7 – Draw some walls

 Click the **Line** tool.

 Make the line thicker.

 Choose dark green.

Use the mouse to draw four walls to contain the maze.

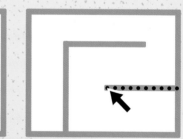

Now add a couple of internal walls to make a very simple maze.

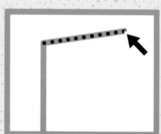

Don't worry if the robot looks too big for the maze, your code will make it shrink to fit.

STEP 8 – Add a target

 Click the **Choose a Sprite** button.

Laptop

Scroll through to find the **Laptop** sprite and click on it.

8

STEP 9 – In position

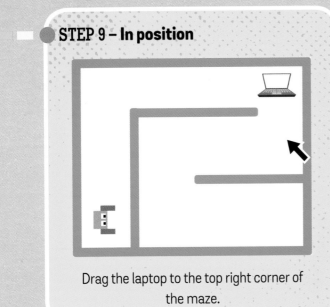

Drag the laptop to the top right corner of the maze.

This will make sure that you are assigning code to the robot.

STEP 10 – Select the robot

Sprite 1   Laptop

Click on the robot to select it.

If the robot is too big, try changing the code to set its size to 30 or 40 percent.

STEP 11 – Code it

Code

Click the **Code** tab. Next, drag the code below into the **Scripts Area** in the order that it is given. This will make the robot move to the laptop.

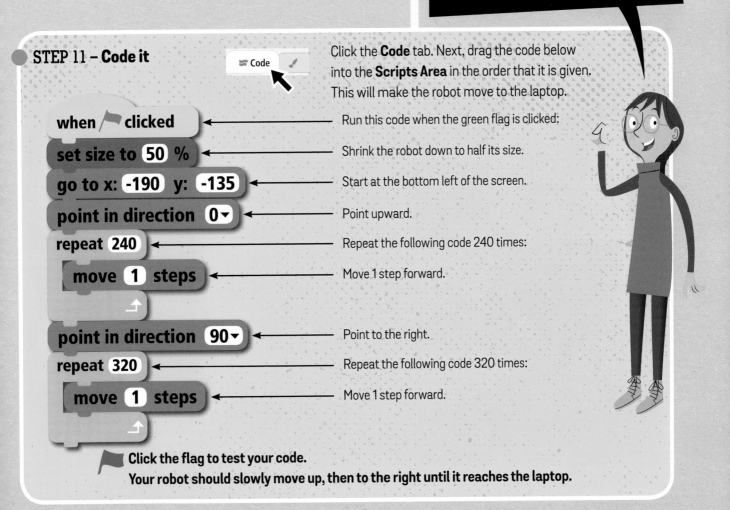

when ⚑ clicked	Run this code when the green flag is clicked:
set size to 50 %	Shrink the robot down to half its size.
go to x: -190 y: -135	Start at the bottom left of the screen.
point in direction 0 ▾	Point upward.
repeat 240	Repeat the following code 240 times:
move 1 steps	Move 1 step forward.
point in direction 90 ▾	Point to the right.
repeat 320	Repeat the following code 320 times:
move 1 steps	Move 1 step forward.

⚑ Click the flag to test your code.
Your robot should slowly move up, then to the right until it reaches the laptop.

Move the laptop sprite to a different part of the maze.

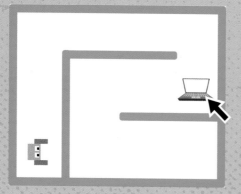

Now click on the robot and change the code to make it reach the laptop in its new position.

Now move it a little farther.

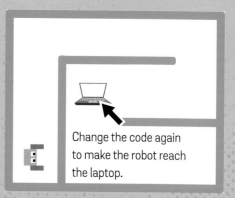

Change the code again to make the robot reach the laptop.

Keep moving the laptop to a new place, then change the code to make the robot find its target.

How it works—moving and turning

Some robots have legs, but most have wheels. Some have caterpillar tracks over their wheels to be able to drive on rough terrain. Wheeled robots usually have two motors, one to drive the wheels on the left and one to drive the wheels on the right.

To make the robot move forward, both sets of motors need to turn clockwise. To make it reverse, both motors turn counterclockwise.

To turn left or right, the motors need to turn in opposite directions. To turn left, the left-hand side motor turns clockwise, and the right-hand side motor turns counterclockwise. To turn right, they do the opposite.

Change your maze by adding more walls. Modify your code so the robot still reaches its target—the laptop.

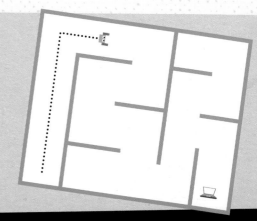

Download more maze backgrounds at **www.maxw.com**

Sensors

So far, our robot has not shown much intelligence. It only found its way through the maze because a prewritten program told it which way to turn and how far to go.

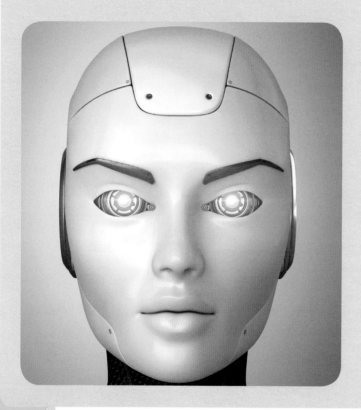

There are many ways to make a robot more useful. One important method is to make the robot more aware of its surroundings. We, as human beings, do this through our five senses. Robots use special components called "*sensors*" to try to detect what is near them.

We can change the code in our maze program to make the robot find its own way. By adding code to make it "sense" where the walls are, it will be able to make choices about when to change direction.

The robot will also need some rules to help it get through the maze. A method called the left-hand rule instructs the robot to try to "touch" the left-hand side of the maze as it moves. A rule in a program, such as this one, is called an algorithm.

Sensing the Way

We are going to make a program that can guide a robot through a maze.

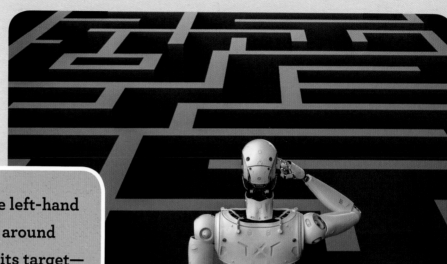

It will use the left-hand rule to move around until it finds its target—the laptop.

STEP 1 – A robot

We need a robot. Use the previous program or follow the instructions on pages 6–7 to draw a new one.

STEP 2 – Add a sensor

The robot will need to check if its left arm is touching the wall. Let's make its left arm act like a sensor.

 Costumes

Click the **Costumes** tab.

Select the **Fill** tool.

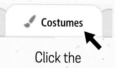

Choose orange.

Color the robot's left arm orange.

STEP 3 – Add a target

Click the **Choose a Sprite** button.

Laptop

Scroll through to find the **Laptop** sprite and click on it.

STEP 4 – A maze

Draw a maze on the backdrop (see page 8 for help).

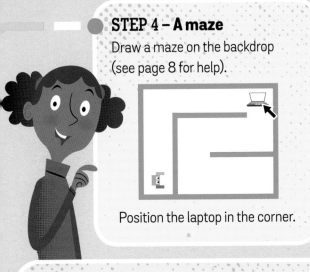

Position the laptop in the corner.

STEP 5 – Select the robot

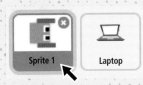

Click on the **robot** to select it.

Picking colors

color is touching ?

Start by clicking inside the square.

Below the color sliders, click on the **Pipette** tool.

Now click on the color on the Stage, such as the orange robot arm and the white background. (The color may change slightly near an edge, so click carefully.)

STEP 6 – Code it!

Click the **Code** tab, then drag this code into the Sprites Area to make the robot reach the laptop. Note: Some code will need to be dragged inside other code.

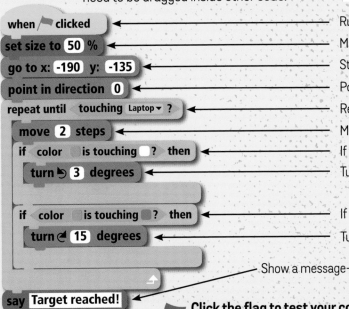

when 🏳 clicked → Run this code when the green flag is clicked:

set size to 50 % → Make the robot smaller.

go to x: -190 y: -135 → Start at the bottom left of the screen.

point in direction 0 → Point upward.

repeat until touching Laptop ? → Repeat the code below until it finds the laptop:

move 2 steps → Move 2 steps forward.

if color is touching ? then → If the left arm (orange) is not touching a wall:

turn ↺ 3 degrees → Turn left toward the wall.

if color is touching ? then → If the left arm (orange) is touching a wall:

turn ↻ 15 degrees → Turn right away from the wall.

Show a message—Target reached!

say Target reached!

Click the flag to test your code. Your robot should make its way through the maze until it reaches the laptop. (If it doesn't work properly, check your code, then try picking the colors again.)

Investigate

Move the laptop around in the maze. Can the robot still find it?

Try drawing a maze that is a different shape. Did the robot make it to its target?

What happens if you change the amount that the robot turns when it finds a wall or white space?

Can you make the robot move faster? Does it still find its target?

13

Taking Orders

Robots can be programmed to do a lot of different tasks.

In this activity, we will draw a robot and program it to do a number of different tasks, including shaking its head, waving, and speaking.

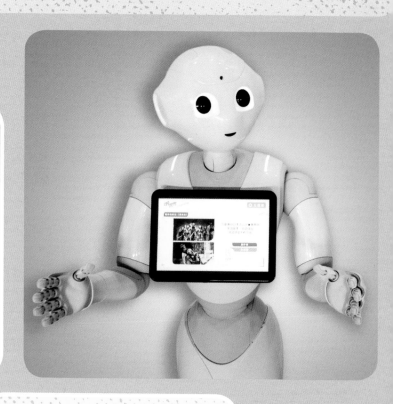

STEP 1 – Remove the cat

Right-click on the cat and click **delete**.

STEP 2 – Add a sprite

Hover over the **Choose a Sprite** button.

Click the **Brush** icon.

For help, go to:
www.maxw.com

STEP 3 – Start drawing

Click **Convert to Bitmap**.

Select the **Rectangle** tool.

Set the rectangle to **Filled**.

Choose a color for your robot.

STEP 4 – Draw the head

Choose orange.

Create a rectangle to be the mouth.

Select the **Ellipse** tool.

Start by dragging out a rectangle about one-quarter of the width of the drawing area in the center.

Hold down the shift key while you draw to make perfect circles.

Drag out two yellow circles for eyes.

Add pupils to the eyes.

Finally, add any finishing touches to the robot's head.

STEP 5 – Draw the body

Draw the main part of the body so that it takes up about one-third of the height of the drawing area.

Make another sprite (see step 2).

Click **Convert to Bitmap**.

Select the **Rectangle** tool.

Choose a color for the robot's body.

Then draw the legs.

Add any extra details.

Once you have completed the body and legs, find them in the Stage area. Click on the head and drag it onto the body so they line up.

STEP 6 – Draw the right arm

Make another sprite.

Click **Convert to Bitmap.**

Select the **Rectangle** tool.

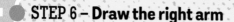

Starting in the center of the drawing area, drag out a simple rectangle for the arm.

> You need to make sure you start drawing the arm in the center of the drawing area. This is where the arm will pivot from.

STEP 7 – Draw the left arm

Repeat the first part of step 6 to make another arm sprite.

This time, start in the center, but drag toward the left to draw the arm.

> You should have four sprites now, like this:

> Drag the sprites around in the storage area so they line up properly. Your robot should look like this.

STEP 8 – Code it!

Click **Sprite1** to select the head sprite.

Click the **Code** tab, then add this code:

when ⚑ clicked	Run this code when the green flag is clicked:
forever	Keep repeating the following code forever:
ask Give me an instruction and wait	Ask the program user to type in an instruction.
if answer = shake then	If the user types in "shake," then run this code:
point in direction 95	Tilt the head slightly to the right.
repeat 5	Repeat the following code 5 times:
turn ↺ 10 degrees	Rotate to the left 10 degrees.
wait 0.1 secs	Wait for a moment (1/10 of a second).
turn ↻ 10 degrees	Rotate to the right 10 degrees.
wait 0.1 secs	Wait for a moment (1/10 of a second).
point in direction 90	Straighten the head.
	Keep on *looping*.

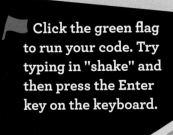

Click the green flag to run your code. Try typing in "shake" and then press the Enter key on the keyboard.

The robot should shake his head!

STEP 9 – Add a sound

Click the **Sounds** tab.

Click **Choose a sound**.

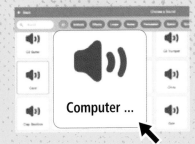

Computer ...

Click **Computer Beep**.

STEP 10 – Change your code

Click the **Code** tab, then add this code at the bottom, just before the end of the "forever" loop block.

if   answer = beep   then
    start sound   Computer Beep ▼

If the user types in "beep," then run this code:

Play the Computer Beep sound effect.

🚩 Click the green flag to test your code. Try typing in "beep" and then press Enter and see what happens.

Now let's give the robot a voice by recording some sound. You'll need a microphone to be able to do this. There may already be one built into your computer.

To let Scratch use your microphone, you need to click the "Allow" button when you start recording.

✓ **Allow**

Beware of other websites asking to use your microphone. Always check with an adult first.

STEP 11 – Robot speech

Click the **Sounds** tab.

Hover over the **Choose a Sound** button.

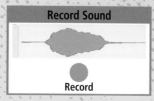

Click **Record**.

Click the **Record button**, then say **"Hello."**

Press **Stop** and then **Save**.

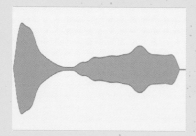

Your voice will be shown as a sound wave like this. Let's add a special effect—the robot one is great!

If no sound wave appears and you can't hear anything, make sure the microphone is selected and turned up. You can check this in the settings program on your computer.

Robot

STEP 12 – Update your code

As with step 10, we need to insert some code to instruct the robot to make a sound. Click the **Code** tab. Add this code at the bottom, just before the end of the "forever" loop block:

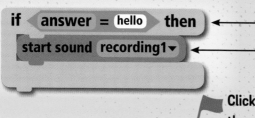

If the user types in "hello," then run this code:

Play the sound recording.

🚩 **Click the green flag to test your code. Try typing in "hello" and then press Enter and see what happens.**

Investigate

What happens if you change the number of degrees turned from 10 to 20 in step 8?

Change the amount of time in the "wait" command block from 0.1 to 0.01. How does this change things?

Try changing the number of times the code repeats from 5 to 10 in step 8. What happens?

STEP 13 – Ask the robot to wave

To make the robot wave, we need to get the head sprite to send a message to one arm sprite.

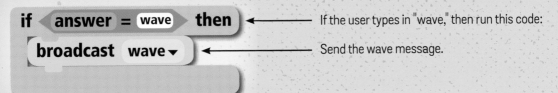

broadcast message1 ▾

Find the
broadcast block.

broadcast message1 ▾

New message

✓ message1

Click **New
message.**

New Message

New message name:

wave

Cancel   OK

Type in **wave,** then click **OK.**

Now we need to insert some code to instruct the robot to send the wave message.
Add this code at the bottom, just before the end of the "forever" loop block:

if answer = wave **then** ◄——— If the user types in "wave," then run this code:

broadcast wave ▾ ◄——— Send the wave message.

STEP 14 – Teach it to wave

Sprite1   Sprite2   Sprite3   Sprite4

In the **Sprites pane**, click **Sprite3**
(the right arm). Drag in this code:

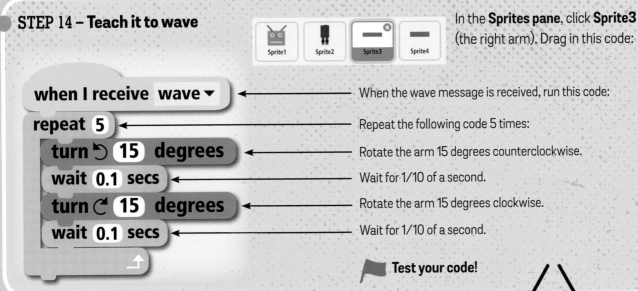

when I receive wave ▾ ◄——— When the wave message is received, run this code:

repeat 5 ◄——— Repeat the following code 5 times:

turn ↺ 15 **degrees** ◄——— Rotate the arm 15 degrees counterclockwise.

wait 0.1 **secs** ◄——— Wait for 1/10 of a second.

turn ↻ 15 **degrees** ◄——— Rotate the arm 15 degrees clockwise.

wait 0.1 **secs** ◄——— Wait for 1/10 of a second.

🚩 **Test your code!**

Code challenge

Make the robot play other sounds, such as new
recorded sounds, when you type different commands.
Don't forget to change the code after adding
new sounds to your project.

Can you instruct it to wave both arms?
You will need to send a new message to both arms.

Teach the robot to wink. Add a second costume
to the robot's head and change one of the eyes.
What else can you make the robot do?

19

The Robot Arm

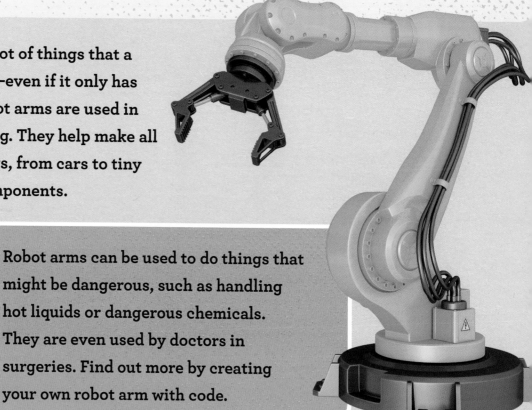

There are a lot of things that a robot can do—even if it only has one arm. Robot arms are used in manufacturing. They help make all kinds of things, from cars to tiny electrical components.

Robot arms can be used to do things that might be dangerous, such as handling hot liquids or dangerous chemicals. They are even used by doctors in surgeries. Find out more by creating your own robot arm with code.

STEP 1 – A robot

Right-click on the cat and click **delete**.

STEP 2 – Add a sprite

Hover over the **Choose a Sprite** button.

Click the **Brush** icon.

Click **Convert to Bitmap**.

STEP 3 – Zoom in!

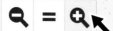

To make it easier to draw the robotic hand, click the **Zoom In** button five or six times to get a closer view.

The drawing area should now look like this. The cross shows the exact center of the sprite.

STEP 4 – Draw the hand

Choose the **Rectangle** tool.

Set it to **Filled**.

Choose a color for the wrist.

Drag out a rectangle. This will act as the wrist for the hand.

Click the **Zoom Out** button twice so you have room to draw the fingers.

Click the **Line** tool.

Choose a color for the fingers.

Make the line a little thicker.

Draw four lines to make the two fingers.

So far in this book we have drawn sprites with the mouse, then moved them around with code. Since the robot arm has two joints that rotate, it will be hard to keep them both lined up if we use sprites. So instead, we will draw the robot arm with code.

STEP 5 – Arm angle

To make the arm move, we need the code to draw it pointing in different directions. The direction it points in will be stored in a *variable*.

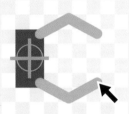

Click the **Code** tab.

Click the **Variables** category.

Click **Make a Variable**.

Type **arm**.

Click **OK**.

For help, go to:
www.maxw.com

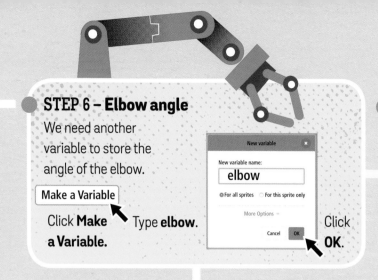

STEP 6 – Elbow angle

We need another variable to store the angle of the elbow.

Make a Variable

Click **Make a Variable.**

New variable

New variable name:

elbow

○ For all sprites   ○ For this sprite only

More Options ▾

Cancel   OK

Type **elbow.**

Click **OK.**

STEP 7 – The pen

We need to add some extra *code blocks* that do the drawing. This group of code blocks is called an extension.

Click **Add Extension.**

Click **Pen.**

Pen

STEP 8 – Code it!

Drag in this code to draw the robot arm.

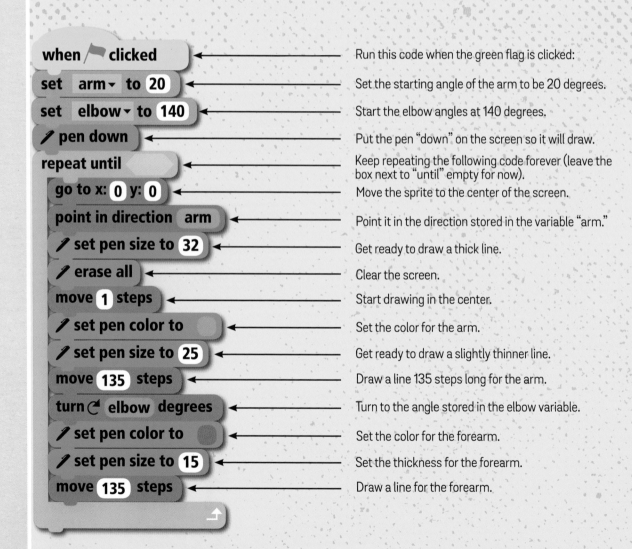

when 🏳 **clicked**	Run this code when the green flag is clicked:
set arm ▾ to 20	Set the starting angle of the arm to be 20 degrees.
set elbow ▾ to 140	Start the elbow angles at 140 degrees.
✏ **pen down**	Put the pen "down" on the screen so it will draw.
repeat until	Keep repeating the following code forever (leave the box next to "until" empty for now).
go to x: 0 y: 0	Move the sprite to the center of the screen.
point in direction arm	Point it in the direction stored in the variable "arm."
✏ **set pen size to 32**	Get ready to draw a thick line.
✏ **erase all**	Clear the screen.
move 1 steps	Start drawing in the center.
✏ **set pen color to**	Set the color for the arm.
✏ **set pen size to 25**	Get ready to draw a slightly thinner line.
move 135 steps	Draw a line 135 steps long for the arm.
turn ↻ elbow degrees	Turn to the angle stored in the elbow variable.
✏ **set pen color to**	Set the color for the forearm.
✏ **set pen size to 15**	Set the thickness for the forearm.
move 135 steps	Draw a line for the forearm.

🏳 **Click the flag to test your code. It should draw the robot arm with the hand at the end.**

STEP 9 – The code

Let's add code to make the arm move.

Pressing different keys will make the arm or the elbow rotate.

when up arrow ▾ key pressed ← When the up arrow key is pressed, run this code:

change arm ▾ by -5 ← Subtract 5 from the value of the "arm" variable.

when down arrow ▾ key pressed ← When the down arrow key is pressed, run this code:

change arm ▾ by 5 ← Add 5 to the value of the "arm" variable.

when left arrow ▾ key pressed ← When the left arrow key is pressed, run this code:

change elbow ▾ by -5 ← Subtract 5 from the value of the "elbow" variable.

when right arrow ▾ key pressed ← When the right arrow key is pressed, run this code:

change elbow ▾ by 5 ← Increase the value of the "elbow" variable by 5.

⚑ **Click the flag to test your code. Pressing the arrow keys will rotate the arm and the elbow joint, moving the robot arm around. Take some time to get used to how the keys work.**

How it works—the robot arm

Robot arms are made of separate sections, just like the bones in our body. Instead of using muscles to move, robot arms have special motors called *servos* that rotate each section. Our robot arm only has two sections, but real robot arms may have six or seven.

A robot arm's fingers or hands often have sensors that can tell when it is gripping something.

Our robot arm is controlled by pressing different keys. Real robot arms are connected to computers that switch the servos on and off to move them. Most computers have specific programs that store instructions for when to activate each servo in order to carry out particular jobs.

Robot Arm Game

We will now add some code to the robot arm to turn it into a game. Apples will appear in *random* positions. See how many you can grab in one minute!

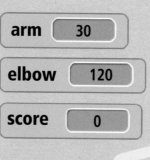

arm 30

elbow 120

score 0

STEP 1 – **Keep score**

Click the **Code** tab.

Click the **Variables** category.

Make a Variable

Click **Make a Variable.**

Type **score.**

New variable

New variable name:

score

● For all sprites ○ For this sprite only

More Options

Cancel OK

Click **OK.**

STEP 2 – **Add a time limit**

Change the main "repeat until" loop to stop the game after one minute.

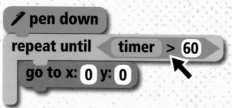

Drag in a "greater than" block from the Operators group. Add a timer block from the Sensing group and type in 60.

Add a message that will show up after the time runs out.

24

STEP 3 – Add an apple

 Click the **Choose a Sprite** button.

 Scroll through to find the **Apple** sprite and click on it.

STEP 4 – The code

 Click on the **Code** tab, then drag in this code to control the apple.

```
when ⚑ clicked                          Run this code when the green flag is clicked:

set score ▾ to 0                        Reset the score variable to zero.

set size to 50 %                        Shrink the apple to half its normal size.

forever                                 Repeat the following code forever:

    go to  random position ▾            Move the apple to a random place.

    wait until  touching Sprite1 ▾ ?    Wait until the robot hand grabs the apple.

    change score ▾ by 1                 Increase the score by 1.

    start sound pop ▾                   Play a sound effect.
```

⚑ **Click the flag to test your game. Use the arrow keys to move the hand around and grab the apples.**

Investigate

Adjust the value by which the arm and elbow variables are changed when keys are pressed (page 23, step 9). How does this affect the way the hand moves?

In the main code (page 22, step 8) change 135 to another number. What does this do to the robot arm?

Code challenge

Change the apple to a different object.

Add a variable called "wrist" that controls the angle of the hand. Update the command keys and main code so the hand can be controlled by other keys.

Adapt the code so that the hand picks up the apple and moves it. You could make another variable called "picked up." Set it to "no" at the start. When the hand touches the apple, change this variable to "yes." Add a new loop that checks to see if the value of "picked up" is "yes." If it is, then use a code block to move the apple with the hand.

The last challenge is very tricky! You need to be experienced at using Scratch and variables to succeed!

Walking and Talking

Robots are growing increasingly similar to humans. One of the most advanced robots was developed by Honda, and is known as ASIMO.

It is just over 4 feet (1 m) tall and has cameras instead of eyes. ASIMO is able to walk and understand simple voice commands. It is even capable of climbing stairs, dancing, opening bottles, and playing soccer!

ASIMO has a complex set of motorized servos, mechanical parts, electronics, and code. It has *gyroscopes* and sensors to help it balance and interact with the world.

Let's create a very simple walking robot using animation and some basic voice control.

STEP 1 – Remove the cat

Right-click on the cat and click **delete**.

STEP 2 – Add a sprite

Hover over the **Choose a Sprite** button.

Click the **Brush** icon.

STEP 3 – Start drawing

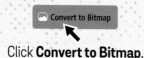

Click **Convert to Bitmap**.

Choose the **Rectangle** tool.

Set it to **Filled**.

Choose a color for your robot.

STEP 4 – Head and body

 Click the Undo tool if you make a mistake.

Drag out a small rectangle to be the body. Start it in the middle of the drawing area, going up.

 Add a head.

 And a neck.

 Make sure your robot is about one-third of the height of the drawing area.

Because we are drawing it as a side view, we will only see one eye.

The bottom of your robot needs to be at the center of the drawing area. If you need to move it, use the Select tool to draw around it. Now click on the robot and drag it into position.

STEP 5 – How fast?

We now need a speed variable to store how fast the robot is moving. (If it is standing still, its speed will be zero.)

 Click the **Code** tab.

 Click the **Variables** category.

Click **Make a Variable**.

Type **speed**.

Click **OK**.

STEP 6 – Stop and go

Drag in this code to make the robot stop or start when the space bar is pressed:

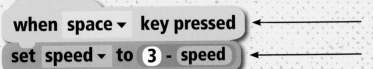

When the space bar is pressed, run this code:

Set the speed to 3 or zero.

27

STEP 7 – Main code

Drag in this code to keep the robot moving.

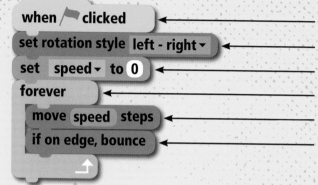

when 🚩 clicked → When the green flag is clicked, run this code:

set rotation style left - right ▾ → Set the way the robot looks when it reaches the edge.

set speed ▾ to 0 → Start with a speed of zero.

forever → Keep repeating this code forever:

move speed steps → Move forward if the speed is not zero.

if on edge, bounce → If it reaches the edge of the screen, bounce and start moving back the other way.

STEP 8 – Add a leg

 Paint

Click the **Brush** icon to make a new sprite.

📷 Convert to Bitmap

Click **Convert to Bitmap**.

Choose the **Rectangle** tool.

We need to begin drawing the leg at the center to make sure it pivots correctly.

Draw a small rectangle. Start in the center of the drawing area, and move down.

Draw a second rectangle at the bottom to create a foot.

STEP 9 – Move the leg

Code

Click the **Code** tab. Drag in the following code to move the leg back and forth.

when 🚩 clicked → When the green flag is clicked, run this code:

forever → Repeat the following code forever:

point in direction 90 ▾ → Start with the leg straight.

repeat 10 ▾ → Repeat this code 10 times:

go to Sprite1 ▾ → Move the leg to Sprite1 (the robot's body).

turn ↺ speed degrees → Rotate the leg counterclockwise. (Using the speed variable means it only turns if the body is moving.)

repeat 10 ▾ → Repeat this code 10 times:

go to Sprite1 ▾ → Move the leg to Sprite1 (the robot's body).

turn ↻ speed degrees → Rotate the leg clockwise. (Using the speed variable means it only turns if the body is moving.)

STEP 10 – Add another leg

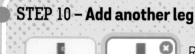

Right-click the leg sprite.

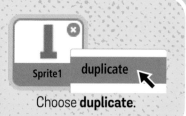

Choose **duplicate**.

STEP 11 – Swap direction

When you duplicate the leg, the code will be duplicated too. But we need this leg to move in the opposite direction to the first leg. To do this, swap the two "turn" blocks as shown below:

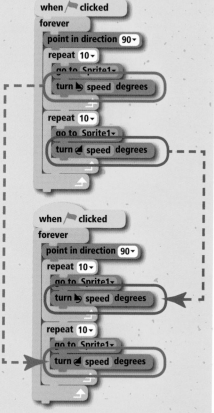

🚩 **Click the flag to test your code. Press the space bar to see your robot walk across the screen!**

STEP 12 – Voice control!

By using a microphone, you can make the robot move when it hears a sound. Add this code, then try clapping your hands to make it move or stop. Try saying "stop" or "go'" and see what happens!

Click the robot sprite.

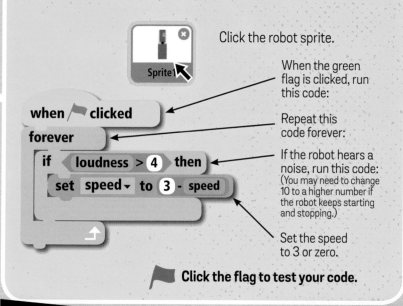

When the green flag is clicked, run this code:

Repeat this code forever:

If the robot hears a noise, run this code: (You may need to change 10 to a higher number if the robot keeps starting and stopping.)

Set the speed to 3 or zero.

🚩 **Click the flag to test your code.**

Your robot doesn't really understand what you say, it just checks whether there is any sound being made. For it to comprehend different words, it would need to analyze the sound in more detail.

See the tips at the bottom of page 17 for help with using the microphone.

Bugs and Debugging

If you find your code isn't working as expected, stop and look through each command you have put in. Think about what you want it to do, and what it is really telling the computer to do. If you are entering one of the programs in this book, check that you have not missed a line. Some things to check:

Join block properly:

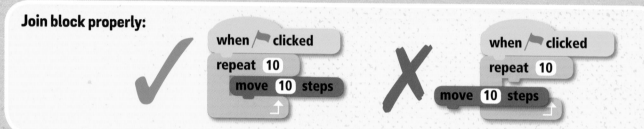

Select sprites before adding code:

Before you add code to a sprite, select it in the **Sprites pane**. This will make sure that the code is assigned to it.

X or Y?

```
set x to 0
set y to 0
```

y   Don't mix
    them up!

The right size

A sprite that is the wrong size may stop your code from working. Use the squares as a guide when drawing sprites. You can always use the "set size to %" code block to make them fit properly.

Right color, wrong code?

Be precise. Many code blocks look very similar, but do completely different things!

Position variables and values carefully:

Don't type in variable names.

Don't just drop them on top of blocks.

Drag them until a circle appears.

The value block will then snap into place.

Tips to reduce *bugs*:

- When things are working properly, spend time looking through your code so you understand each line.

Experiment and change your code. Try out different values.

To be good at *debugging*, you need to understand what each code block does and how your code works.

- Practice debugging! Make a very short program and get a friend to change one block only, while you aren't looking. Can you fix it?
- If you are making your own program, spend time drawing a diagram and planning it before you start. Try changing values if things don't work, and don't be afraid to start again—you will learn from it.

Glossary

algorithm	Rules or steps followed to make something work or complete a task
bug	An error in a program that stops it from working properly
code block	A draggable instruction icon used in Scratch
debug	To remove bugs (or errors) from a program
degrees	The units used to measure angles
gyroscope	An instrument with a turning wheel, mounted on an axis that can turn in any direction
icon	A small, clickable image on a computer
loop	Repeating one or more commands a number of times
random	A number that can't be predicted
right-click	To click the right mouse button
sensor	A device that measures something in the real world, such as the temperature, and sends it to a computer as a value
servo	A special motor in a robot that can turn very accurately
sprite	An object with a picture on it that moves around the stage
stage	The place in Scratch that sprites move around
steps	Small movements made by sprites
system	A combination of software, hardware, sensors, and information
variable	Part of a program that stores a value that can change

Index and Further Information

FURTHER INFORMATION

Gifford, Clive. *Awesome Algorithms and Creative Coding.* Crabtree Publishing Company, 2015.

Wainewright, Max. *Code Your Own Games!: 20 Games to Create from Scratch.* Sterling Children's Books, 2017.

Wainewright, Max. *I'm a Scratch Coder.* Crabtree Publishing Company, 2018.